Christine Jolee Ashley (nee WATSON)

42, Llwynon Cres
Oakdale

BLACKWOOD YESTERDAY

in photographs
including the villages of
**WATTSVILLE, CWMFELINFACH, YNYSDDU,
PONTLLANFRAITH, OAKDALE, CEFN FFOREST,
ARGOED AND MARKHAM**

Ewart Smith, M.Sc.

Book 1

OLD BAKEHOUSE PUBLICATIONS

ABERTILLERY

First published in June 1991

ISBN O 9512181 6 6

Published in the U.K. by
Old Bakehouse Publications
Church Street,
Abertillery, Gwent NP3 1EA
Telephone: 0495 212600 Fax: 0495 216222

Made and printed in the U.K.
by J.R. Davies (Printers) Ltd.

Contents

Foreword by Alun Pask
former British Lion and Captain of Wales

Many of our valley towns have seen publications which relate to their pictorial history and which give a comprehensive record of the development of their industrial, commercial, religious, educational and sporting past. This latest book by Ewart Smith certainly brings back to me many personal memories of our heritage and of the proud history of Blackwood and its surrounding villages.

I have known the author many years both as a good friend and as a teaching colleague. His knowledge of Blackwood's history is indeed extensive and for years he has researched and collected old photographs, a significant number of which are now presented in book form for everyone to enjoy.

Looking through the book certainly brought back many memories. I saw faces I had not seen for over thirty years. Names came flooding back, shops and buildings stirred memories of my childhood and schooldays, and once I began reading the book I could not put it down.

I am sure that this book will give tremendous pleasure to many residents and former residents of the Blackwood area when they recall 'the good old days'. One photograph in particular, the VE Celebration Party at Albion Terrace, brought back vivid memories of the wonderful community spirit that existed in those days.

The younger and newer residents of our area will, I am sure, also appreciate and take pride in the heritage depicted in such marvellous photographic style. I am always proud to say that I was born and bred in Blackwood and I wish Ewart every success with his latest publication. I hope he will continue to record, in such permanent form, his vast knowledge of Blackwood and its history.

Congratulations on an excellent book which, I am sure, will find its way into very many homes.

Alun Pask

Acknowledgements

Very many people have helped in the production of this book, through their willingness to share information and by the provision of many old photographs, specific details of which are listed below. On occasions it is difficult to determine the 'facts'. Any errors that occur must be considered wholly mine, and for these I apologise. In particular I would like to thank the County Archivist, Mr. Delwyn Tibbot M.A. and his staff for their help, and for permission to reproduce parts of the maps referred to below. My greatest thanks must go to Mr. Gwilym Davies of Old Bakehouse Publications, Abertillery, who initiated this book and kept a careful eye on its production at every stage. I must also thank his staff who have always been most courteous and helpful, and who have made many worthwhile suggestions.

My grateful thanks are due to the undermentioned who kindly loaned original material from their own collections, and who helped to identify faces and places and provided dates and other interesting details.

Mr. & Mrs. Cam Bennett (130,168,170,185,187,217,218), Mr. & Mrs. Russell Bennett (142,156,163), Blackwood Rugby Club (138,139), Mrs. Eileen Bowen (124,177), Mrs. M. Bray (78,79,159,171), Mr. Tom Brown, Cefn Fforest Junior School (88), Mr. Billy Constance, Mrs. P. Croker (12,165,166,208), Mr. & Mrs. Idwal Davies (91,94,97), Mr. & Mrs. Jack Davies (83,184), Mr. Max Davies (129,144), Mr. Richard Davies, Mr. Byron Farr (92,179), Mr. Arthur Griffiths (133), Gwent County Archives (2,3,5,196), Mrs. O. Hemmings, Mr. Haydn Howell (150,151), Mr. & Mrs. Roy Hunt (82,90,99,126,146,149), Mr. & Mrs. Arthur Jenkins (113,157,169,175,183), Mr. Cyril Jones (20,55,70,100,119,123,145,174,199), Mrs. Doris Lewis (158), Mrs. Edna Lewis, Mrs. Eileen Lewis, Mr. Gwilym Lewis, Markham & District Band (160,161), Mr. Elvert Morgan, Mr. Jack Morris (38,195), Mr. & Mrs. Reg Nash (7,155,173,215), Mr. Alun Pask (140), Mr. & Mrs. Owen Parfitt (85,86,147,167,181,186,188,209), Mr. Jack Perry (180), Mr. & Mrs. David Price, Mr. Tony Read-Gibbs (Blackwood Golf Club - 141,143), Mr. Gary Rosser (89,93,95,98,153,154,164), Mr. Gordon Rosser (Blackwood Cricket Club - 134,135), Mrs. Julie Silcocks, Mr. Watkin Tasker (201), Mr. & Mrs. Arthur Thomas (77,80,81,105,121,122,214), Mr. Elwyn Thomas (48,172), Mr. Bill Tippins (125,128), Mr. Graham Walker (84,131,132,148,182), Mr. Les White (178), Mr. Clive Williams (136), Mr. & Mrs. Evan Woodward (137,212,213).

Introduction

Prior to the Sirhowy Tramroad, which was opened in 1805, it is safe to say that no buildings existed in the area we now call Blackwood. The map of 1801 giving the planned route of the tramroad shows a bridge over the river at the Rock (Pont Syr Dafydd), the Gelly Dowill farm (still operational), Maesyryryd farm (Maes Manor), Ty'r Graig (possibly Rock House near the entrance to the golf club), a bridge near the Rock and Fountain Inn (Pontynis pwll du), together with Plase (Plas Bedwellty) and Penllwyn - homes of the ubiquitous Morgan family. Coed Duon (The Black Wood) was bounded by Libanus in the south, the lane that is now Hall Street and Cefn Road on the north, the River Sirhowy to the east and Plas farm on the north. There were no mines and the only language was Welsh.

Much of the early development of Blackwood must be attributed to John Hodder Moggridge of Woodfield. John Moggridge was born at Bradford-on-Avon, Wiltshire, in 1771. Moggridge's family inherited an estate in Dymock, Gloucestershire, where they became the local gentry, culminating in Moggridge's appointment as high sheriff of that county in 1829. Shortly afterwards he sold up and bought the Rhos-newydd estate in this area from Miss Mary Morgan, the last of the family that had influenced almost everything that had happened in this region for several centuries. Moggridge's estate of approximately 450 acres straddled the Sirhowy river and included the areas known as Plas, Penmaen & Llys Pentwyn, Woodfield, Cwm and Glan Braenar (see map). Plas was the only area in the parish of Bedwellty, the remainder of the estate being to the east of the river in the parish of Mynyddislwyn. In 1827 he wrote an article to a periodical known as *The Oriental Herald* under the title of 'Interesting Settlement in Wales - an account of the principles and progress of an experiment for

1. The view across the Sirhowy river standing in front of the Rock and Fountain Inn, c. 1918. The white cottages, known as Powell's Houses, are typical of those initiated by John Moggridge between 1820 and 1830, although they would originally have had stone roofs. The house on the right was a gas works' house and was much later.

improving the condition of the labouring classes of society, in the hills of Monmouthshire'. The article makes extremely interesting reading, the editor commenting that such ideas could well be taken up by 'the influential people of India'.

In the early days of the nineteenth century times were very bad for the 'labouring classes' and around 1820 things had taken a turn for the worse, resulting in many poor but hardworking souls abandoning everything they had in this country to seek a new life in America or New Holland - a former name for Australia. In response to the degradation, wretchedness and poverty around him Moggridge decided that he should try to do something that would give the people some independence and self respect, and would stimulate an altogether happier way of life that would benefit, ultimately, the whole community. He proposed grants of land for a term of any three generations (later extended to four) on condition that

1. The tenant should pay a regular but moderate ground rent.
2. The tenant should personally assist in the erection of a substantial and commodious cottage. However, his efforts should not interfere with his regular work.
3. Any money advanced by Moggridge should be secured by the premises, and repaid by instalments at regular intervals.

Moggridge decided that one eighth of an acre would be a suitable area for each house and garden and that the annual ground rent should be about 20 (old) pence a year i.e. about 8p. This fee, which was less than the annual rent for cottages in the neighbourhood, included the privilege of securing stone from the local quarries and timber for the roof from nearby woodland. In addition the tenant was expected to cultivate his garden and was allowed to keep the produce. The spot assigned for this experiment - the only part of Moggridge's estate to the west of the Sirhowy river - was part of a wood of one hundred and five acres shown on maps of the time as Y Coed Duon (The Black Wood). This area was sheltered from the westerly wind and rain by a densely wooded hill while on the other side of the valley stood Moggridge's recently built residence of Woodfield. The selected area was dry and healthy, and possessed good soil, with springs of pure water gushing from the hill on the west. It was intersected by a railway or tram road joining the Tredegar iron works and adjacent collieries with Newport. A good carriageway ran alongside the tramroad and the two banks of the river had just been connected by an iron bridge of one arch. It seems that this is the Rock and Fountain bridge, marked on maps of the day as Pont ynys pwll du, and still in use today. Timber was to be left standing where it would not overshadow or otherwise harm the garden. The ground would be cleared at the expense of the landlord and an acre of ground near the centre of the village was set aside to become the village green - a beautiful area shaded by mature oaks and beeches.

From the many prospective tenants three only accepted Moggridge's initial offer. In the spring of 1820 these three built their cottages and planted their gardens with leeks and onions. Potatoes were almost unknown in this area then. By the summer of 1822 nearly forty such plots had been leased, a significant reason for taking up these leases being the value of the home-grown fruit and vegetables. Each newly built house contained an upper room to let as lodgings to single men - of whom there were many who had come to work in the nearby collieries and levels. Each cottage had its own oven in the chimney corner of the living room. The cost of the lease plus the ground rent was between forty-five and fifty shillings (£2.25-£2.50) a year. This figure was chosen so that it was less than one third of the

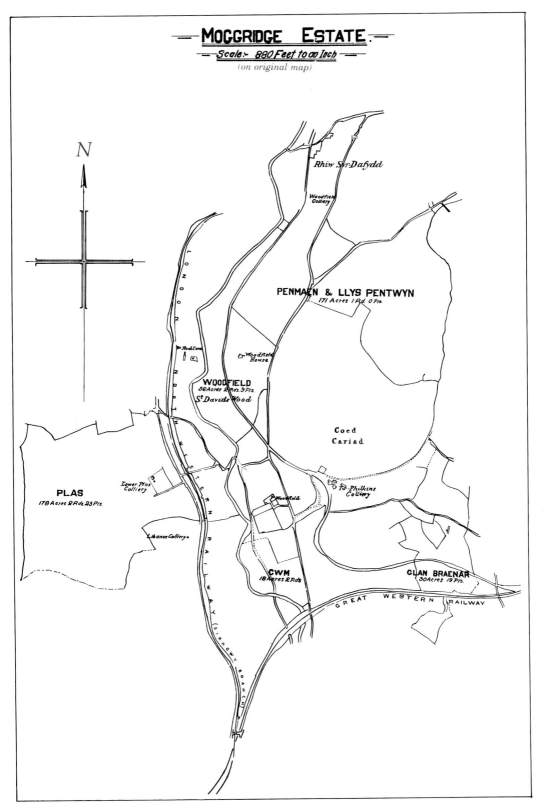

2. A plan of the Moggridge Estate after the railway had been re-routed around the back of the High Street. Blackwood began in the area marked Plas which extended to the river.

7

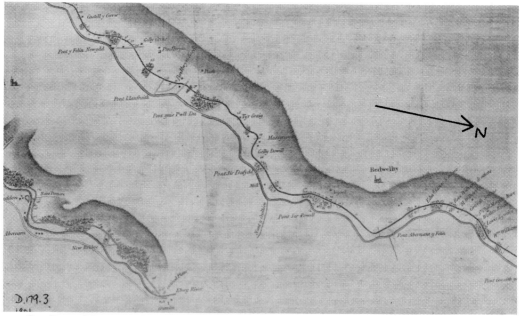

3. Part of the 1801 plan of the proposed Sirhowy Tramroad from Tredegar to Newport.

anticipated total receipts from lodgers. Each householder should therefore make a clear profit of about £10. In addition a market house was opened on 30 October 1822 (on ground to the north of The George Hotel) and its long room was used in all manner of ways. After Moggridge licensed it for divine worship in 1823 a host of different denominational groups met there, as did the village Provident Society (est. 1824). Newspaper reports of the time referred to the village by the name of Tre-Moggridge. How would we have liked our town to be called by that name?

As the years passed more leases were offered and taken up every year until 1827 when there was a seven week stoppage in the local mines due to 'a depression in the state of trade'. The mineowners wanted a reduction in wages and the ordinary working man was not prepared to accept. While the strike went on those who had built their own cottages spent much of their time tending their gardens and when Moggridge returned to Woodfield after some time in London they expressed their desire to return to work but sought his protection from the other, more militant, groups in the area. It was seven weeks before they all returned to work and the leasing and building of new cottages began again. By 1828 there were 260 houses and 1550 inhabitants in The Black Wood. An inn of some capacity had been erected (The Royal Oak), two surgeons were resident in the village (one of these was certainly at Myrtle Grove above St. Margaret's Church), apart from general shops, a baker, a butcher, a gardener, a glazier, shoemakers, tailors, carpenters, masons, sawyers, tilers and last but by no means least, a schoolmaster. From 1827 the market house long room was used for day and evening classes. Up to 200 adults and children were taught there daily. Apart from the lack of education another problem was the lack of a place of worship for the influx of English folk, who, by now made up four-fifths of the inhabitants. Early in 1828 the long room was fitted out as a chapel and a bell installed. They used the liturgy formulated by Samuel Clarke, chaplain to Queen Caroline. A chapel library was also established at a cost, to borrowers, of a penny a week. It is an ill wind that blows no one any good. The 1827 strike did help many people appreciate that they could do a great deal to help themselves.

Moggridge's local, social experiment was seen as a great success, so much so that a few miles down the valley the village of Ynysddu (The Black Island) was born in a similar way. More than thirty houses were built in Ynysddu - most of them being better than those in Blackwood! Likewise, as a result of an Act of Parliament (1825) permitting the making of a road from the Bute Works, Rhymney, running through the area, more than fifty houses were built at Trelyn (Town pool, and now part of Fleur de lys) over the hill from Blackwood. By 1829 the total population of the three villages was around two thousand. The name of the mother village was by now firmly established as Blackwood.

Without question Moggridge's social experiment brought advantages to the ordinary people of the area but it should not be allowed to pass without comment that the greatest benefactor was Moggridge himself. He recorded that the total rents from his estate increased significantly as did its saleable value. Furthermore, as the law stood then all the properties built on Moggridge's estate would belong to his heirs after four generations. A most important consequence of this social experiment was that a core of the most talented and industrious workmen became tied to the area. These folk lived in cottages they had built themselves so were most unlikely to leave them. They were also keen to live in a law abiding community, some even becoming special constables in the strike of 1827. They provided the skills so necessary to the continued expansion of coal mining in the area.

In the 1990's we tend to think of Blackwood High Street as a dangerous place to be, and there are times when you take your life in your hands simply to cross the road. We tend to believe that things were much better one hundred and fifty years ago. Certainly we would believe that life on Blackwood High Street was safer and quieter in 1843 than it is today, but such a belief would be untrue. What follows is based upon a report that

Woodfield Bridge.
Sirhowy River,
Blackwood.
1293.

4. Woodfield Bridge over the Sirhowy river at Blackwood. On old maps this crossing point is marked Pont Ynys Pwll Du. Jerusalem Chapel and the graveyard are visible on the left, while the Rock and Fountain Inn is just out of view to the right. Tipping has taken place, probably in an attempt to prevent flooding. The photograph was taken in the 1920's. To this day the bridge remains single track.

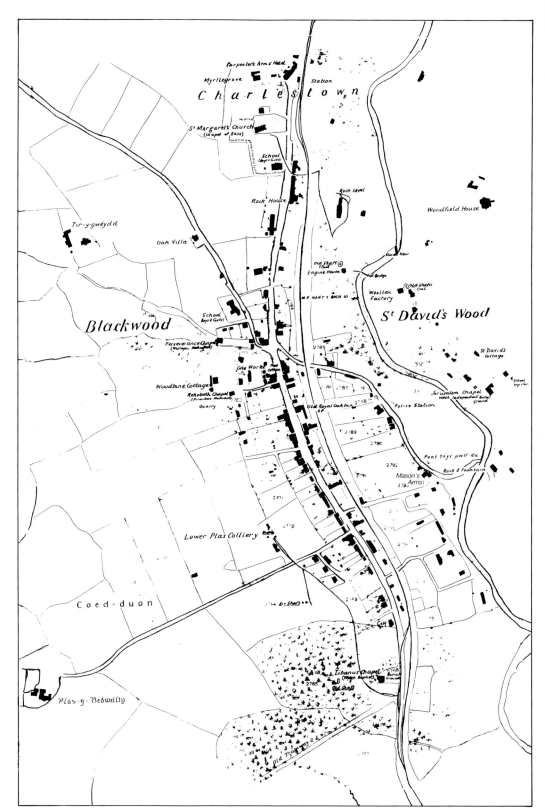

5. Part of the 1880 Ordnance Survey Map, showing the region from Libanus in the south to the station in the north. The area north of The Square in Blackwood was called Charlestown.

10

appeared in the *Monmouthshire Merlin,* one of the influential newspapers in the county at that time.

Picture an old widow sitting at a table in a cottage opposite the George Hotel on a Saturday afternoon in April 1843. She was drinking tea, as many widows are apt to do, and watching the world go by. The Vulcan steam engine, belonging to the Tredegar Iron Company was slowly chugging along the main street outside her window hauling its load of empty trams towards Tredegar. It stopped near The George, possibly for the engine driver to obtain some liquid refreshment. Suddenly there was a mighty explosion, such as no one in the village had ever experienced before. The boiler of the engine fractured. Two bystanders, William Davies, a farmer of Buttry Hatch and Philip Williams of Blackwood, were killed. Williams died instantly, and Davies, an octogenarian, within three hours. They had been engaged in a conversation with Mr. D. Lewis, a shopkeeper, who was severely wounded. Every square of glass, both at the back and the front of The George was shattered by the explosion and part of a roof of a coach house adjoining the hotel was blown off. The two cottages on the other side of the road, one of which housed the widow, had all their windows blown out, but by some miracle the old lady, together with her cup of tea, was untouched. A certain James Hale was also most fortunate to escape - he was sitting on the fore plate of the Vulcan when the explosion took place, causing a large piece of the boiler to fly over his head. So powerful was the explosion that a piece of pipe three and a half feet long and weighing one hundredweight was blown over the house and picked up some four hundred yards away.

An inquest was held most promptly at the Royal Oak Hotel next door, being conducted by the coroner William Brewer. A verdict of accidental death was returned, but Samuel Homfray agreed to pay all the costs incurred as a result of the explosion. This included £40 for new windows - a not inconsiderable sum for those days. The value of the engine was estimated at £500. What a day in the history of Blackwood that must have been. Stand opposite The George some time and imagine exactly what went on.

The town

6. General view of Blackwood in 1911. Pentwyn Road is being laid and the first house in South View Road (The Lindens) being built. Coronation Road has been completed while Albany Road is in process of construction. Both streets were built by Ebden.

7. Red Lion Row, Blackwood. Part of a row of six houses adjacent to the Red Lion Inn and now a car park. Behind them (the chimneys are visible) were two back-to-back houses with one room up and one room down. Each house in Red Lion Row was two up and two down with a stone staircase winding around the chimney.

Blackwood, from the fields. 1302.

8. The bottom end of Blackwood from Woodfieldside, pre-1920. Gordon Road runs from the centre of the picture to the skyline. Lilian Road is on the right with spoil from Lower Plas Colliery in front of it. This is the site of the new 'bus station.

BLACKWOOD. MON

9. Looking west from Woodfieldside towards Blackwood. The Mason's Arms, with its quadrant retaining wall of beautifully dressed stone, features in the centre of the photograph. The Beech Tree is prominent on the skyline.

10. General view of Blackwood from the railway line at Woodfieldside, c. 1925. The Capitol cinema (now Kwiksave) is behind the trees in the centre of the picture. The twin gabled house on the left together with the terrace to its right (Highland Place) were demolished to make way for the new market complex. The large tree on the horizon, slightly left of centre, is the Beech Tree, a famous land mark to older inhabitants.

11. Entering Blackwood High Street from the south, c. 1910. The Parrot Hotel advertises its stabling while two heavy horses harnessed into a four-wheeled cart are standing outside the ironmongers. They suggest a heavy load.

12. The south end of Blackwood High Street in the late 1950's. The shops on the right hand side are Crokers, the outfitter (later Lennards and now Talk of the Town), Palmer the butcher (later Jack Rogers and now Philip's Hair Salon), and Houghton's, the radio and cycle dealer (later Hextalls radio and television and now The Cane Shop).

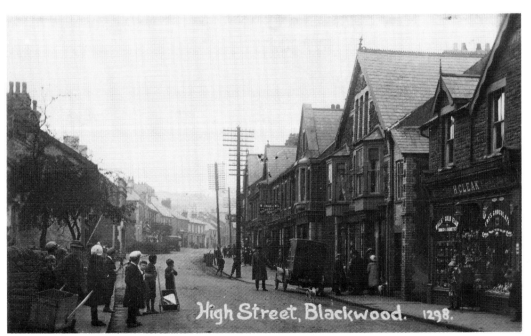

13. This pre-1920 scene on Blackwood High Street shows Cleaks, the well known high quality sweet shop. The building adjacent to it was demolished to widen the road at the top of Bridge Street. Norman Lewis advertises his Painless Dentistry. Trees and gardens were still a feature of the High Street.

14. The white building adjacent to the Tredegar Industrial and Provident Society building, and the terrace beyond, have long since disappeared from this 1910 view of the south end of Blackwood High Street. They have been replaced by the Post Office and Belle Vue Discount, the furniture, carpet and electrical store.

15. High Street, Blackwood, in the early 1950's. The site has been cleared but the new Post Office has yet to be built.

16. High Street, Blackwood, c. 1950. Apart from the Maxime cinema and Embassy ballroom most of the buildings visible on the right hand side have disappeared. The opposite side of the High Street is structurally unchanged.

17. Blackwood High Street, looking south, c. 1912. This Post Office was built by Miss Watkins who had taken over the village post office from the Edmunds brothers. It became a Crown office in the spring of 1917. There was a telephone exchange at the rear and a sorting office in the basement. The three permanent staff were Miss Watkins (the postmistress, who hailed from Pontypool), Miss Williams (Radnorshire) and Miss Bennett (Bargoed). Mr. Radford was the postman. At that time any female employee of a Crown Post Office was forced to resign on getting married.

17

18. The Post Office, High Street, Blackwood, in the early 1920's. J.H. Murrin is the newsagent next door to the Post Office, which is now Currys. A group of whitewashed cottages can be seen further along the street. They are built well below the level of the road. Their troughings are beneath the ground floor ceiling level of the adjacent Star Supply Stores. A small garden in front is guarded by iron railings.

19. An early view of Blackwood Post Office. In front of the Post Office is a red telephone box and a 'Stand for 5 buses'. Next to the Post Office is Tudor Evans, the ironmonger and supplier of colliery tools. A Morris van is able to make a three-point turn outside Lambert's the Clothiers with consummate ease.

20. The east side of Blackwood High Street c. 1968. Few of the businesses on this stretch of the High Street are still operating.

21. A very early picture of the High Street. There was no need to worry about traffic when crossing the road in those days. Just below the 1d Bazaar is The Butchers Arms, now The Porters.

19

High Street, Blackwood.

22. The centre of Blackwood High Street in 1909. Williams & Co., Provision Merchants, was to become Templeman's, the radio centre. On the other side of the lane, which now leads to the Market Square, was F.J. Twissells. The large building high up in the centre of the picture was The Rink, a multipurpose building constructed from corrugated sheeting and used for films, slide shows, boxing, roller skating and general entertainment. It was the social mecca of the town, the main entrance being up narrow wooden steps from the High Street at a point between Stevens Value and the public toilets. The entrance is still detectable.

23. The centre of Blackwood looking north, c. 1915. Beer barrels rest on the pavement outside the Royal Oak. The message on the rear of this card describes the town as 'a pretty place with glorious hills'.

24. Blackwood High Street looking towards The Square c. 1928. The Forresters Hotel advertises Billiards (not snooker!) while the Royal Oak opposite offers stabling. Next along the High Street is Prince's the draper, originally the site of J.V. Lewis, Grocer and Baker. This site subsequently became Rees the Bon, The Empress Restaurant, The British Restaurant during World War II, and is now Lambert's the Clothiers.

25. The two shops nearest to us on the right hand side belong to E. Cromwell Jones, Grocer and Wine Merchant, and J.D. Roberts, Outfitter and Draper. The block was built around the middle of the last century by Richard Morris, who also had a bakehouse at the rear. Between this building and the single storey building beyond was a narrow lane known to locals as 'Morris Lane'. This led to the Primitive Methodist Church now The Little Theatre. The heavy balustrade on the building opposite surmounted the premises of A.P. Hughes, Draper & Milliner. A.P. Hughes sold out to The London Hosiery Company, one of the conditions of the sale being that he should not open in competition elsewhere in the town. Every problem has a solution! He got around this by providing financial backing to Bill Jones (his draper) and Miss Richards (his milliner) and thus was born Jones & Richards - the shop that was to become 'The Fashion Centre of the Valleys'. This business easily outlived The London Hosiery.

26. The Square, Blackwood, c. 1912. What freedom of the roads there was for pedestrians in those days.

27. The Square, Blackwood, c. 1914. A pillar box has recently arrived. A mother and child survey the scene from a balcony above the National Provincial Bank.

28. Blackwood High Street from The Square, c. 1950. The stone balustrade at the front of The London Hosiery had been a problem for some time and is being removed from wooden scaffolding. The belisha beacon on the edge of the narrow pavement outside Glanfrwd House (now the site of Woolworths) marked the position of a pedestrian crossing. No zebras then!

29. The Square, Blackwood, 1932. Wick Thomas' Central Cafe or Milk Bar was a well known meeting place. The iron railings next to the gas standard are part of an important landmark. They surround the underground 'gents'. What treasures are buried there! The pillar box is in its original position.

30. Miners' Welfare Hall, Blackwood, opened in 1926.

31. A small problem with snow on Blackwood High Street, March 1947. This was probably the worst winter on record.

32. The Cenotaph, Blackwood, in 1926. The road layout shows that plans for the council estate, which was not erected until after World War II, were in mind then.

33. The Cenotaph, Blackwood, in 1970, from the north. How the trees around it have grown.

34. Gordon Road, Blackwood, c. 1914. Hazeldene, the detached house on the left was the residence of the Scudamore family. They had a bakery, grocery and provisions business at the top of Bridge Street. The old bakery building is still there, including the projection for the pulley system which allowed bags of flour to be raised to the upper floor. William Diamond, estate agents, holds the site at present.

35. A scene at Gordon Road, Blackwood (said to be named after General Charles George Gordon of Khartoum), just after World War I.

36. William Street, Blackwood, 1910, showing clearly how the 'ashes' were left for the council workmen to collect. In some areas collections took place every day.

37. The Weir, Blackwood, c. 1920. This is to be found a short distance upstream from the footbridge near Sunningdale Nurseries.

38. Cwmgelli, Blackwood, looking north from the bend on the Foundry Hill. The railway line, including the bridge, is now the line of the main road. The sidings have vanished and been replaced by lawns and flower beds. The old main road, Tredegar Road, has become a cul-de-sac. The sheds on the left of the photograph show the position of Treharne's Iron & Brass Foundry.

39. Pentwyn Avenue, Blackwood, c. 1930. The last plot awaits development. On the left are the tall trees of the church woods. The houses in the distance are part of South View Road.

40. The Beech Tree, Blackwood, c. 1910. This beautiful tree dominated the western skyline above the town. It was struck by lightning in a storm in the early 1930's.

41. Today we know this as Cwm Gelli Farm, but old maps show numerous spellings, e.g. Gellidewyll, GellyDowill and Gellidowilt.

CHAPTER 2

The surrounding villages

42. Two blocks of semi-detached houses at Wattsville, together with a terrace of four and a terrace of three. Each house has a large garden in front, but on the opposite side of the road. The two boys wear long trousers and caps on a warm summer's day and stand beside their prize possessions and principal mode of transport. The man carries goods in his wicker basket.

43. Duffryn Street, Wattsville, 1908. More money has probably gone into the construction of these houses than most others in the vicinity. Note the beautifully moulded bricks around the windows and doorways, the finely cut stone pier caps and the intricate ironwork.

44. Commercial Street, Wattsville 1908. Taken from the north looking towards Crosskeys. The older houses are on the right hand side while those opposite are slightly larger and with more impressive front windows.

45. Commercial Street, Wattsville, 1907. The same row of houses as in picture 44 but viewed from the south. Almost everyone has a head covering. Note the gas standard in the foreground.

46. Glanant Street, Cwmfelinfach, 1910. The principal means for the transport of goods at that time was the horse and cart. The son, with his sister on his lap, looks after the horse and cart while his father sells milk from a churn. Next door down stands a mother with her baby wrapped in Welsh style. The pavements are well laid but it will be some time before the tarmacadam road is added.

47. Commercial Street, Ynysddu, c. 1910. Dando's ironmongery and general shop is on the left hand side with a large wicker skip and a two-wheeled truck outside. A bowler-hatted father sits on the front step supervising his daughter at play. The unmade road is most uneven.

48. Ynysddu from the east, c. 1908. The shop belongs to Hughes the grocer. The new road has yet to be constructed behind the houses in the foreground.

49. Wyllie Village from Ynysddu. The village was built to house the labour force for Wyllie Colliery. This deep mine was opened by the Tredegar Iron and Coal Company in 1926 and closed in 1967.

50. The Mill, Gelligroes, in the 1950's. This ancient building is believed to originate in the 16th century. It is T-shaped, part single and part double storey, has stone tiled roofs and two divided 'stable' doors. The water wheel is one of the overshot type, with iron framed buckets. From this site the first radio signals in the area were transmitted and received by the Moore brothers. Old seats from Bedwellty church found their way into the interior of the mill and an original Victorian letter box is still in use in the west wall.

51. Islwyn Terrace, Pontllanfraith, from the south west, c. 1914 (shown on the postcard as Elim Road!). This is on the route from the Plough corner to the open air baths.

52. Sir Ivors Road, Pontllanfraith c. 1910. This is the present main road from Pontllanfraith to Newport. The original main road was along Gelligroes Road which is behind the houses on the left.

53. Penmain Road, Pontllanfraith c. 1916. The Plough Inn is visible in the distance. Short trousers have now become the fashion for boys!

54. The Old Monastery at the Big Penllan Farm, 1930. Today it is known as the Penllwyn Hotel.

55. Penllwyn Sarff, a 16th century stone tiled, two-storey Tudor mansion with wide square headed windows, moulded mullions and drip moulds. This beautiful old house, now The Penllwyn Hotel, was built, together with Rhos Newydd (The Plas Inn at the top of Gordon Road) by Thomas Morgan for his youngest and favourite son, Edmund. Thomas fought with the Earl of Richmond at the Battle of Bosworth in 1485 and was rewarded with a grant that allowed him, among other things, to buy the parishes of Bedwellty and Mynyddislwyn.

56. Mynyddislwyn Council Offices (with cupola), Bryn Road, Pontllanfraith, in the 1950's. Tredegar Junction Station, in the distance, now sports an overhead footbridge. This has been installed to enable pedestrians to cross the line while the level crossing gates are closed for the trains to pass. The War Memorial in front of the Council Offices has been removed and now stands in front of the new Islwyn Borough Council Offices a little distance north of this spot.

57. A warm early morning spring day in Pentwynmawr High Street. A mother and baby, together with a hen, can walk peacefully in the middle of the road. The white cottages, with their low ceilings, are typical of the homes built in these valleys in the previous century.

58. The bowling green and tennis courts at the Welfare Ground, Cefn Fforest, Blackwood, c. 1950.

59. The Old Village, Bedwellty, in the mid 1920's. Two men stand outside the New Inn. The school is a little further along the road.

60. The Park, Cefn Fforest, Blackwood, in the mid 1920's. This park, bounded by Bedwellty Road on one side and Harry's Hill on another, provided the most favoured route for the many folk who walked between Blackwood and Bargoed.

61. General view over Cefn Fforest from the south east. The giant Aberbargoed tip can be seen in the distance, behind the trees. Bedwellty indoor baths have been built in the open space to the left of the wood.

62. Oakdale Colliery in the 1950's. The modern village of Oakdale looks down on the older settlement at Rhiw Syr Dafydd.

63. Oakdale Hospital soon after its opening in 1914.

64. Central Avenue, Oakdale, c. 1938, looking south west from the village green.

65. The Square, Oakdale, in the early 1950's. The centre of the village was beautifully kept. Well stocked flower beds can be seen at each end, together with closely cut lawns between them.

66. West View Crescent, Oakdale, 1917. This crescent was built to house Oakdale Colliery officials.

67. Syr Dafydd Avenue, Oakdale, c. 1925, with Oakdale Post Office on the right. The road leads to the schools and to the pit entrance.

68. Oakdale Terrace, Penmain, c. 1930. This is the main road between Blackwood and Oakdale.

69. Looking along Penmain Avenue towards Oakdale Post Office in 1930.

70. Cwm Corrwg or Cwm Argoed, in 1963. The white building in the foreground is the Castle Hotel, to its right are the Flannel Factory and the Corn Mill, both of which were water powered. To the left are Island Street, built in 1901, and Greenfield Street. Over the Cwm bridge, Pont Sir Powell on some old maps, James Street is on the right. The ruins of Sir Thomas Phillips' Colliery School can be seen on the left above the railway line. Built in 1841 this was the first works' school in Wales supported by a government grant. In addition Sir Thomas established a lending library, built a new church, set up a cooperative store in conjunction with the colliery, and promoted a 'sick' fund.

MKM 9   ABERNANT ROAD, MARKHAM.

71. A view of Markham looking north from the top end of Abernant Road.

CHAPTER 3

Education

72. Pontllanfraith Schools, c. 1910. This building was almost completely destroyed by fire in 1911.

73. The Pontllanfraith Schools soon after reconstruction.

RHIW SIR DAVID COUNCIL SCHOOL, OAKDALE.

PUB. BY CHIVERS,
OAKDALE POST OFFICE.

74. Rhiw Syr Dafydd Council School, Oakdale, built in 1908, the year Oakdale Colliery opened. This photograph shows the extension in the process of construction.

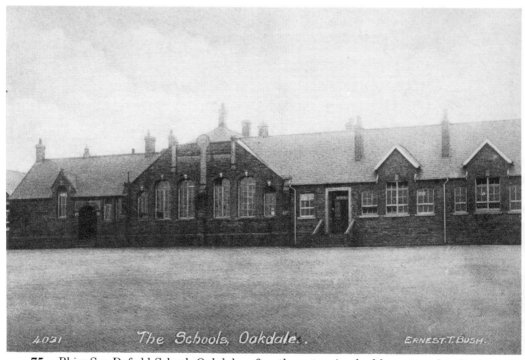

4031   The Schools, Oakdale.   ERNEST T. BUSH.

75. Rhiw Syr Dafydd School, Oakdale, after the extension had been completed.

76. This large modern school, on Pentwyn Road, was built before the First World War because the school on Cefn Road became too small to accommodate all the children in the area. Subsequently the Cefn Road school was used exclusively for infants. Pupils attended the new school until they were old enough to leave. The buildings became part of the comprehensive school until the new school was built at Ty Isha Terrace.

77. Blackwood Infants' School, class 1, 1922. The teacher is Miss Annie Nethercott.

78. Libanus School Infants, 1927.

79. Libanus School Juniors, 1927.

80. Blackwood Infants' School, Cefn Road, Class 1, 1927.

81. Blackwood Junior School, Pentwyn Road, 1927. The teacher is Mr. Hough. Note the gas lighting.

82. Pupils at Blackwood Junior School, 1960.

83. Miss Lyn Humphries with some of her evacuee children. A trainload of evacuees arrived at Blackwood Station on 2nd June 1941. Many residents still have a vivid picture of the crocodile of youngsters carrying their cases and gasmasks to the hall from which they would be chosen by those who would look after them. The infants went to New Tredegar, the juniors were billeted in Blackwood while the pupils of Dover County School were taken to Blaenavon.

84. Third year pupils at Libanus Junior School, 1951. The teacher is Miss J. Jones.

85. Enthusiastic pupils at Cefn Fforest School, c. 1948. Gwyn Lewis, Michael Jones, Patsy Capewell, Gary Lewis, Mary Capewell, Sian Lewis, Valmai Norman, Catherine Jones, Janet Jones, Mary Davies.

86. The members of the cast of a Nativity Play at the Central Methodist Church in the 1970's. The cast includes, from the left: Lyn Couzens, Rachel Morris, Nia Parfitt, Helen Phillips, Audra Burton, Robert Thomas, Adrian Edwards, Michael Howells, Stephen Horler, Nigel Game, Mark Watkins and Peter Game.

87. Third year pupils at Cefn Road School, Blackwood, in 1941. Every child was instructed to carry a gas mask, hence the diagonal straps across most of these children. A gas attack was greatly feared at this stage of World War II.

52

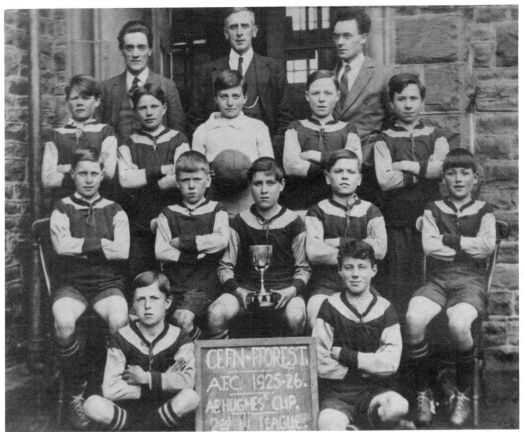

88. Cefn Fforest School soccer team 1925-26. They won the A.P. Hughes Cup (A.P. Hughes was a local draper and milliner) and finished second in the league.

89. Pupils at Pontllanfraith Technical School in 1945. The headmaster is Mr. Dick Vines.

90. Pontllanfraith Grammar School's leading athletes and sporting stars with Mr. Roy Hunt and Mr. George, the headmaster, in the 1950's.

91. Pontllanfraith Grammar School Rugby XV, 1953. Apart from the headmaster Mr. Cliff Rowlands and Mr. Walter Sweet (extreme right) the photograph includes the future Welsh International and British Lion Alun Pask (standing fourth left).

92. Pontllanfraith Grammar School's First Rugby XV, 1955-56. Back row: Carl Thomas, Robert Williams, Philip Jones, Dawson Phillips, Derek Mills, Michael Ellis, Geoff Morris. Second row: Mr. Roy Hunt, Michael Price, Byron Farr, Geo. Jenkins, David Evans, Robert Dearth, Mr. J. Capewell. Seated: Anthony Llewellyn, David Jenkins, Byron Thomas (capt.), Dennis Harris, David Moore.

93. Blackwood Secondary School staff, 1966. Back row: P. Davies, W. Hutchings, P. Giles, J. Palmer, O. Parfitt, A. Williams, D. Brooks, R. Owen. Third row: E. Evans, Mrs H. Bolwell, Mrs. P. Rosser, Miss A. Salway, Mrs. N. Davies, Mrs. C. Lewis, I. Davies, A. Morgan, R. Jenkins. Second row: B. Hardwick, Mrs. B. Bennett, Mrs C. Metcalf, Miss E. Jones, Mrs. E. Evans, Mrs. V. Nutland, Mrs. M. Westcott, Mrs P. Jenkins, D. Bond. Front row: H. Moses, Mrs. N. Vaughan, Miss J. Jones, C. Cannan, R.T. Jones (headmaster), Mrs. I. Hilditch, Mrs. K. Hamilton, Mrs. M. Walters, A. Wilkins.

94. Pontllanfraith Grammar School prefects 1953-54. Head Boy John Musselwhite, Head Girl Joyce Thomas. The headmaster is Mr. Cliff Rowlands.

95. Members of Blackwood Secondary School, on the occasion of a visit to the Houses of Parliament in July 1960. Mr. Howell Moses' party was met by Mr. Harold Finch, the Member of Parliament for Bedwellty.

96. Girl prefects at Pontllanfraith Grammar School, 1953. Standing: Hazel Cummings, Molly Maquire, Helen White, Pam Saunders, Tracey Winterson, Avril Hughes, Shirley Gwilt, Jean Hambleton. Seated: Maureen Hunt, Hazel Williams, Mr. C. Rowlands (headmaster), Pam Houghton, Joyce Thomas.

97. A visit by the pupils of Pontllanfraith Grammar School to The Houses of Parliament in 1953 accompanied by, left, Miss England and right, Mrs. Hibbins, Miss Bowditch, Miss Phillips, Mr. Harold Finch M.P. and Mr. Cliff Rowlands.

98. Blackwood Comprehensive School staff, 1975. The headmaster is Mr. J. Powell.

99. Pontllanfraith Grammar School's First XV 1947-48. Captain Bob Todd is sitting between Mr. J. Capewell and Mr. Walter Sweet.

CHAPTER 4

Religion

100. Cwrt-y-bela Church from the west. This church, dedicated to Saints Philip and James, after Sir Thomas Phillips and his wife, whose maiden name was James, was built in 1857 and witnessed its last service in 1969.

101. Bedwellty Church, c. 1945.

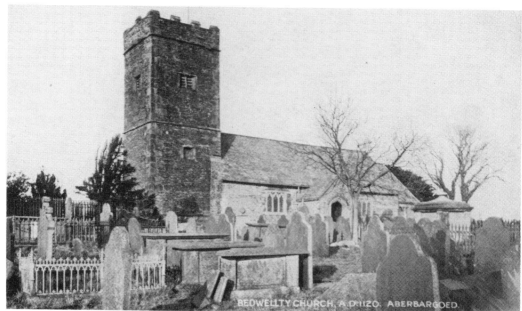

102. Bedwellty Church is the most westerly ancient parish church in Gwent. The origin of the name is somewhat obscure, one suggestion being that it means 'Wellte's dwelling'. The church is dedicated to St. Sannan, an Irish saint contemporary with our patron saint, St. David. Robert de Haia made a grant of the church to the Abbey of Glastonbury in 1101. Although the building was in a state of disrepair at the beginning of the 13th century, the present church dates from c. 1220. The church was extended in the 14th century when the embattled beacon tower was also added. A most interesting feature of the inside of the church is the set of mason marks exposed where the respond facing the chancel has been removed from the original set of four. Against the north chancel wall is the jewel of the church, an intricately carved oak vestment chest, c. 1450. An iron tombstone on the path to the south porch is dated 1778; a small headstone near the east gate records the death of Catherine Dillin in 1859 at the ripe old age of 110; Thomas Ellis, the famous engineer, and designer of some of the very first steam engines used in this country, is buried on the west side; and a grave to the south records the deaths of five children under 5.

103. Bedwellty Church altar and organ c. 1925.

104. Bedwellty Church from the south in 1908. There are several points of interest: a water cart, a traction engine on the road to the right, and a little girl with a donkey.

Old Vestment Chest
with unique Carving.

Old Fount,
Bedwellty Church.

105. This picture shows the old vestment chest, c. 1450, and the old font, as photographed in 1902. The upper side panel of the chest depicts two pierced hands and a heart, and two pierced feet, surrounded by a crown of thorns. On the lower half, in the centre, is a shield with three nails. Surrounding the shield is a scourging whip, a hammer and a spear.

106. The parish church of St. Tudor, Mynyddislwyn, from the east, c. 1908. Tradition informs us that an earlier building was erected on a site a little way away. This collapsed mysteriously at night on two occasions. As a consequence the builders kept watch and during their vigil they heard a voice saying 'Myned is a llwyn', which means 'go below the bush'. There has been a church on this site from at least 1101 for Robert de Haia granted the church to the Abbey of Glastonbury in that year. The present building is largely the result of a rebuilding that took place in 1819-20.

107. Mynyddislwyn Church showing the east window with three cinque foiled lights. This window is filled with modern stained glass depicting Mary and Martha at the Resurrection, and was installed prior to World War I. An amusing memorial tablet inside the church tells us that a certain John Williams died in the year 17,783, the unfortunate stone engraver cutting the second 7 instead of an 8. Islwyn's last bardic chair was given to the church in 1925 by his only surviving niece.

108. Libanus Baptist Chapel, c. 1904. This Welsh chapel was opened in 1830, the name Libanus meaning 'Biblical Place'. The first meetings of its members had, from about 1825, been held, with John Moggridge's blessing, at the Blackwood Market Hall. Slowly but surely the influx of English folk into the area began to strangle the Welsh language and in 1861 Mount Pleasant Baptist Church was established for English speakers. As time passed Libanus became anglicised and eventually the members there joined with those at Mount Pleasant. Some years ago the building underwent a change of function. It remains within the Baptist cause as a Christian community centre.

109. New Bethel Chapel and Monument, Mynyddislwyn, 1908.

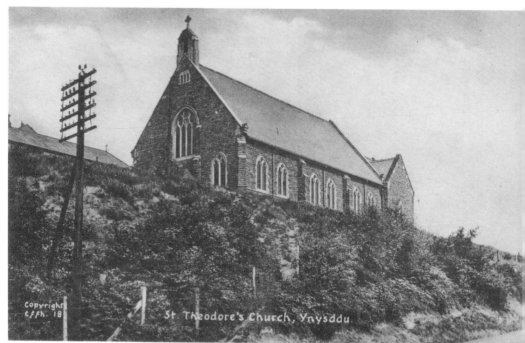

110. St. Theodore's Church, Ynysddu.

111. A happy group of Mount Pleasant Sunday School scholars pause briefly outside the Crown Inn in the early 1950's. The Crown Inn and the adjacent newsagents were kept by Ceph Stewart. The newsagents (known to many as Court's) became Rowlands, and Tescos was built on the Crown site. The corner shop (now Seth Phillips the estate agent) was Jones & Richards wool shop at that time.

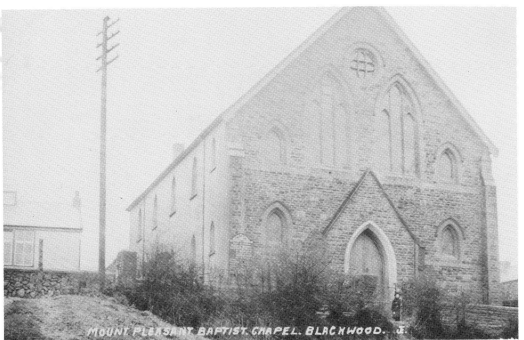

112. Mount Pleasant Baptist Church, Cefn Road, Blackwood, in 1908. The origins of this church go back to 1861, when half a dozen English-speaking Baptists left Libanus. Because they had no meeting place they were continually moving around. First they met at the old Wesley Chapel, then in the school room of Jerusalem Congregational Chapel, next in the chapel at Maesycwmmer, then in a house at Dandy Row near the Red Lion Inn, followed by the club room of the Parrot Hotel and finally at the Chapel of Ease at Cwmgelli. By 1881 they had bought a parcel of land in Cefn Road and immediately erected a single storey school room on it for £350. The present chapel was built at a cost of £1500 and was opened on 6th March 1892. In the 1930's the school room at the rear became a two storey building. The 'tin' shed to the left was used by pupils from Pentwyn Road as a cooking centre and later a canteen. The infants moved to the new school at Apollo Way about ten years ago.

113. Mount Pleasant Baptist Choir, June 1920. The conductor is Mr. Thomas Norman. This photograph is taken at the rear of Pentwyn Road School.

114. Wesley Chapel, Blackwood. This chapel, seating a congregation of 630 was opened on 9th November 1898, and replaced the Perseverance Wesley Chapel that had stood on the same site since 1861. It cost £1250 to erect and served Wesleyans well until a disastrous fire on the evening of 23rd November 1915 razed it to the ground. It was to be 1928 before a new church was built on a new site nearer The Square.

115. The Wesleyan Church, Blackwood, in the late 1920's. It was better known as The Central Methodist Church and, because of its size and choir facilities, was the usual venue for choral concerts.

116. Members of the Central Methodist Church taking part in the 1950 Whitsun march along Blackwood High Street.

117. Central Methodist Girls' League Choir, 1927. Back row: Myra Parsons, Eileen Knott, Lily Williams, Gladys James, Olive Gregory, Elsie, Mrs. W. Davies (Bryn Celyn, president), Molly Woodward, Bessie, Gladys Norman. Second row: Stella, Sallie, Emily, D. Cooper, Doris, Mrs. G. Burden (conductor), Jennie Sheen, Edith Jones, Renne Sumption. Front row: May Eyles, Hilda Gregory, Gertie Williams, Phyllis Deere, Gladys Jones, Unknown.

118. Jerusalem Independent Chapel.

119. Argoed Baptist Chapel. This is one of the oldest chapels in the area still in regular use.

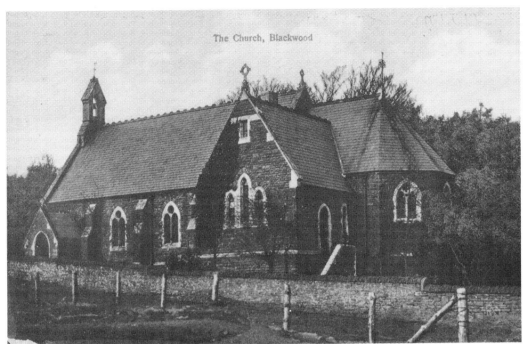

120. St. Margaret's Church, Blackwood, from the south east, c. 1913. The posts and fencing show the boundaries of the New Rock Colliery which was a working deep mine at the time.

121. Part of the Whit Monday Procession of Witness, c. 1951. To the left of Vicar Ellis Evans is Sam Davies, the church organist at St. Margaret's for more than 45 years: to his right is John Bennett, father of Mark who has become so successful in the world of professional snooker. The cross bearer is Arthur Bennett, John's father.

122. St. Margaret's Girls' Friendly Society garden party held at the Vicarage in 1924. The vicarage at that time was Bryntirion, Bloomfield Road. The clergyman is Rev. Luther Evans. He was appointed the first vicar of Blackwood in 1921.

123. Rock Calvinistic Methodist Chapel. This chapel and dwelling house was built, and opened in 1839, principally as a result of the efforts of Evan Jones of Llangeitho, Cardiganshire, the master of the nearby Bedwellty School.

124. St. John's Church, Markham, built in 1927 to serve the needs of the 370 houses in the new village. The first incumbent was Rev. Rhys Davies. In spite of additional building in the village the church was forced to close due to lack of support. It was taken down in the 1980's.

125. A gathering at St. Sannan's Church, Bedwellty, c. 1955. The clergymen and lay readers from the left are: Mr. David Pritchard (lay reader), Bishop Edwin Morris (Bishop of Monmouth), Rector (later Canon) James Davies, Rev. Bernard Fry (curate), Mr. Wilfred Moore (lay reader), Mr. Hemmings (lay reader), Mr. Roberts (lay reader).

CHAPTER 5

Sport and Entertainment

126. Presentation of the Swimming Awards by Mr. Musselwhite at Pontllanfraith Swimming Baths, 1968.

Pontllanfraith Baths, Blackwood, Mon.

127. Pontllanfraith Open Air Swimming Baths. During World War II, and subsequently, pupils used to walk from Blackwood along the old tramroad to these baths for swimming lessons.

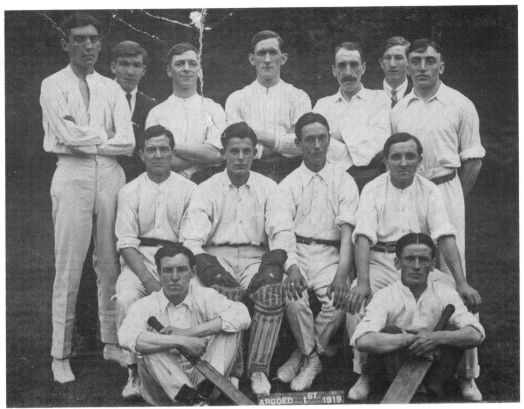

128.   Argoed Cricket Club in 1919.

129.   Cefn Fforest Welfare A.F.C., 1955. This team won the Monmouthshire Senior League and were the Monmouthshire Challenge Cup winners. Standing: W. Quarry, R. Perkins, K. Hancocks, C. Flowers, T. Williams, J. Williams, R. Neale, H. Holloway, R. Wallace, W. Walters (trainer). Seated: G. Price, H. Howells, G. Turner (capt.), G. Simmonds, D. Weeks, M. Davies.

73

130. Blackwood Bowling Club in the late 1950's. Standing: Len Brown, Vicar Clements, Ivor Hanes, Cam Bennett, Bill Heaton, Bill Granville, Gwyn Pask, A. Bryant, David Harvey, Reg Jones. Seated: Tom Bromley, John Morris, John Perkins, Jack Morris, Haydn Jones, Harold Williams, Bill Coleman, Arthur Pratlett.

131. Joe Walker delivering his wood in front of the old clubhouse at the Showfield in the early 1950's.

132. The Trundlers on their annual bowling tour of the south coast in 1968.

133. The presentation to Arthur Griffiths of a board and set of chessmen to mark the occasion of his becoming the first Welsh Champion when Welsh Championships were introduced in 1953. Arthur was top board for Blackwood Chess Club for many years. Standing: Unknown, Arthur Parfitt, Theo Szary, Geo. Jones, Henry Golding, George Snow, Unknown, Charlie Saffin, A. King, David Price, Owen Morgan. Seated: Chairman of the Miners Welfare Institute, Reg Jones, Arthur Griffiths, Ned Evans.

134. Blackwood Cricket Club, First XI, 1957. Standing: A.J. Jenkins, N. Purnell, W. Taylor, H. Davies, R. Gwilt, A.R. Jenkins, R. Gwatkin. Seated: A.J. Jenkins, C. Bosley, J. Evans, K. Parfitt (capt.), A.R. Parfitt, R.R. Parfitt.

135. Blackwood Cricket Club, Second XI. Winners of the Third Division of the league in 1980. Standing: Eric Reardon, Colin Morgan, Steve Jones, Bob Smith, Jeff Mudford, Steve Parsons, Dorian Waite (scorer). Seated: Mike Samuel, Derek Daniels, Brayley Reynolds, Ray Meader, Mal Ford.

136. Members of Blackwood Tennis Club at their headquarters at the Showfield in the late 1950's. Back row: Nina Prosser, Bob Elmes, David Hoyle, John Lewis, Chas Scrivens, Alan Edwards, Haydn Howell, Ian Edwards, John Bray, Marie Jones, Dorothy Constance. Seated: Shirley Jones, Ann Hardwick, Mrs. Elmes, Bill Brain, R.H. Edwards, Esq. J.P., (president), Brian Hardwick, Margaret Alderman, Lucy Richards, Valerie Keddle. Juniors: Michael Davies, Windsor Royall, Norman Gatehouse, Ian Lewis, Terry Winters.

137. A group of greyhound enthusiasts gathered in front of Chappell's stables which were behind the present Argus Office on Blackwood High Street c. 1930.

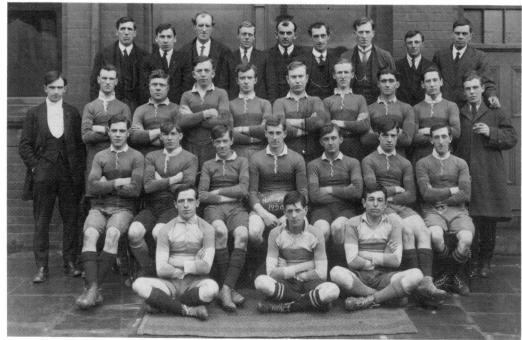

138. Blackwood Rugby Football Club, 1920-21. Back row: H. Prosser (treas.), H. Gibbs, W. Perriman (chairman), J. Lewis, G. Perkins, B. Bradford, F. Lease, D. Lilly, H. Pope (hon. sec). Third row: T. Parry, L. Brown, B. Bradfield, A. Brimble, H. Holvey, J. Crew, L. Evans, P. Jenkins, A. Prosser, L. Bennett (capt.). Seated: B. Watkins, B. Garrett, D. Carter, R. Vaughan (vice-capt.), S. Bartlett, J. Holvey, T. Harris. Front row: W. Cobley, A. Bendle, S. Dunford.

139. Blackwood Rugby Club First XV during their very successful 1950-51 season. Back row: R. Harris, H. Tovey, B. Moore, T. Harper, G. Fletcher, T. Bowen, S. Bond, S. Lewis, J. Hart. Seated: D. Dyer, V. Simmonds, E. Evans (capt.), C. Bosley, C. Jonathan, C. Russell. Front row: P. Medway, J. Morgan, R. Liddington, N. Liddington.

As far as can be ascertained from newspaper accounts the first recorded rugby match in Blackwood was against Bargoed at the Tramroad ground, part of Woodfield Farm, on 19 January 1889. Blackwood, captained by D.L. Richards, won by 3 goals, 2 tries and 2 minors to 1 try. Included in this team were a local doctor (Howell Evans), the proprietor of the local lodging house (Bowen), a member of the family owning the Rock Foundry (J.E. Treharne) and two members from the Moggridge family of Woodfield House, the seat of the local gentry.

The club was founded in 1893 by a group of employees from Treharne's foundry who had gathered for this purpose at the Carpenters Arms, just north of St. Margaret's Church. Away matches were played against Blaina, Bargoed, Brynmawr, Aberbeeg and Tredegar while all the home matches were played at the Tramroad pitch.

In 1895 an unfortunate accident took place in a Second XV home game against Aberaman. William Reynolds fell awkwardly and was buried beneath a heap of players. He suffered a serious spinal injury and died a few days later. This, compounded with the fact that Mr. Watkin Walters, the owner of the ground, lost his wife in a smallpox epidemic, resulted in fixtures being abandoned for almost a year. When they restarted, home matches were again played on the Tramroad ground. This continued until 1906 from which time the Showfield was used.

Without question the best years for the club were in the 1930's. In 1935 almost 5000 spectators witnessed the first floodlit rugby match in Wales when Blackwood took on Crosskeys at the Showfield. Glanyrafon Park became available in October 1935 after the Bedwellty Urban District Council had spent twelve months preparing it, and from 1936 to 1940 Blackwood were undefeated at home. This success continued after the war, a particular highlight being that achieved by the 1950 side. Captained by Edgar Evans they captured Cardiff Athletic's post-war ground record.

The present day well appointed clubhouse was originally built as a Police Station and Law Courts, and subsequently became the local headquarters of the Royal Ancient Order of Buffaloes, before being purchased by the club with the help of Courage Breweries. New changing rooms have recently been built on Glanyrafon Park. Originally the club played in black but c. 1930 it was thought that a brighter image was required. As a result the present club colours of black, red and amber were adopted.

Today, the club is successful both on and off the field, the First XV being well established in the Third Division of the league. The chairman, Owen Parfitt and the secretary Allan Lewis, together with all officers and members of the club look forward to the future with confidence and enthusiasm.

140. Alun Pask, captain of Wales for the first time, scoring the try against England at Twickenham on 15th January 1966 that enabled Wales to win by 11 points to 6. In spite of losing to Ireland in Dublin, Wales went on to retain the championship for the first time in 57 years.

141. A group of notable Blackwood citizens photographed with Cwmgelli Farm and Oakdale Colliery in the background. These gentlemen are possibly the founding members of Blackwood Golf Club, but many of them were involved in numerous other organisations that thrived in and around the town. Blackwood Golf Club was formed in 1914. The first clubhouse, a simple building of corrugated zinc sheeting painted green, was destroyed by a fire in the early hours of St. David's Day 1964. A new clubhouse was opened by Mr. (later Sir) Harold Finch M.P., in 1966 and an additional lounge area added in 1979.

142. Blackwood Golf Club's fortieth anniversary celebrations, 1954. Seated: H.S. (Ches) Rees, Ken Jones (hon. sec.), Ted Lewis (founder member), D.J. Thomas (founder member), Leslie Evans (chairman), George Vaughan, Mrs Nancy Jones, D. Hilton Lewis (clerk to Bedwellty Council).

143. One of the most outstanding personalities in the history of Blackwood Golf Club was Miss Rachel Lewis of Ty Isha Farm shown here in 1929. She became a member of the newly founded Ladies' Section in 1921 and was the first Lady Captain of the club in 1927. At her best she played off a handicap of 8. She was still playing regularly some fifty years after her initial successes.

144. Cefn Fforest Cricket Club 1921. B.H. James (sec.), S.Rudge, A. Davies, D. Williams, J. Lane, D. Higgins, D. Davies, E. Partridge, C. Miller, G. Davies (treas.). Seated: A. Cookshaw, A. Wallace (capt.), G. Lane, C. Jacka. In front: P. Davies, L. Smith, J. Rosser (vice-capt.).

CHAPTER 6

Memorable events

145. The cast and orchestra of the musical Gypsy Love at Argoed Institute c. 1930.

146. St. Margaret's Church Dramatic Society. The cast of the Easter Passion Play, 1957.

147. A group of dancers at the Welfare Hall, Blackwood, attending a Chamber of Trade dance in the 1950's.

148. Blackwood Boys' Brigade (First Company) Soccer Team, 1950-51. Rear: David Howley, Keith Richards, Owen Parfitt, Gwilym Walker, Clive Davies, Glyn Amesbury, Mr. Cliff Porch. Front: Colin Alderman, Bryan Gerrett, Keith Jones, Arthur Morgan, John James.

149. The cast of St. Augustine's Church, Pontllanfraith, musical production in the mid 1930's.

150. The cast of Zureika The Gypsy Maid which was performed at Markham Institute, in the late 1940's.

151. Markham Welfare Institute Junior Choir, 21st March 1951.

152. The cast of Alcestes, c. 1942. Blackwood Dramatic Society staged this production in the courtyard of Maesrhyddyd House. This photograph was taken in what is now part of the Maes Manor Hotel ballroom.

153. The interior of the Capitol cinema, Blackwood, c. 1950. The building was originally used for live shows and as an indoor market before it became a cinema.

154. Mr. Rosser, the manager, welcoming members of the audience at the Capitol cinema, Blackwood, in the early 1950's.

155. Raymond Parker of Dandy Row, which was opposite the present Red Lion car park. He was a page boy at the Maxime cinema when it opened c. 1936.

156. The cast of Blackwood Operatic Society's production of Maid of the Mountain, April 1951.

157. Boys' Brigade camp at Saundersford 1950. Standing: Mr. S. Hutton, Keith Jones, Bill Jenkins, Brian Thomas, Arthur Jenkins, Mr. Cliff Porch, Unknown, Bryan Gerrett, Colin Alderman, Gwilym Walker, Mr. Fred Brooks, Mr. Joe Walker. Seated: Mr. Harry Riley (captain), Mr. Harry Griffiths, Mr. Albert Vittle, Mr. George French. In front: John James, Eddie Williams, Ron Jones, Barry Purvis.

158. Blackwood Girl Guides at camp in the 1950's. The officers include Miss Lil Davies (capt. Fleur de lys), Mrs. V. James (capt. Oakdale), Mrs J. Jones, Miss Doris Davies (capt. Blackwood) and Mrs. Charlotte Powell M.B.E., (President of the Local Association).

159. Members of a weekend course for Rovers and Rangers, held at Blackwood Secondary School in 1961. Back row: Unknown, Robert Wade, Penry Jones, Howard Roberts. 3rd row: Mr. Beavan, Graham Cross, Cynthia Jeffries, Glyn Hankin, Granville ?, Unknown, Julie Bray, Mary Lynne Jones, Pat Pask, Unknown. 2nd row: John Grayson, Rhys Hankin, Fluff, Jackie Jones, Ernie Monk, Pam Carroll, Veronica Morris, Jane Whatley, Jennifer Jones, Pat Flowers. Seated: Terry Christopher, Mary Beavan, Barbara Jones, Alec Morgan, Audrey Jeremiah, Grenville Coleman, Unknown.

160. Markham & District Colliery Silver Prize Band. Back row: T. Davies, T. Bills (treas.), R. Morris, T. Walton, H. Davies, A. Spencer (committee). Middle row: E. Jones (drum major), D. Price (bandmaster), H. Morgan, N. Burton (asst. bandmaster), H. Phillips, D. Jones, G. Sadler, D. Davies, G. Price, G. Eynon, L. Hamer, C. Walton. Front row: J. Powell, W. Davies, T. Morris, S. Hughes, B. Maloney, Miss P. Evans, R. Hamer, C. Price, B. Reynolds, W.R. Hamer (chairman), G. Evans (secretary), V. Evans.

Markham British Legion Band was formed in 1928 and held its first rehearsals in a tin shed behind a cafe in Markham. It became the Markham and District Colliery Band in 1930 and, by the time the Second World War had started, had achieved considerable success. At that time it was ably supported by Markham Miners' Welfare Institute and by an active Ladies' Section who organised many functions, including carnivals and comic football matches, to raise badly needed funds. After the war it took a long time to get going again but by 1958 the band had achieved Championship standard. In 1967 the band moved into its own band room and in 1968 was the Champion Band of Wales. The following year they were the only civilian band to play at the Investiture of H.R.H. Prince Charles.

A freak storm in January 1976 completely destroyed all their music and uniforms. The long haul back started with the formation of a Junior Band at Blackwood Comprehensive School and gradually things improved. The culmination was the opening, a few years ago, of a new band room at the Showfield, Blackwood. Since then they have gone from strength to strength. They now have a full complement of bandsmen and have returned to Championship standard. The band has competed in numerous National Brass Band competitions, winning many first prizes, and have performed at The Crystal Palace, The Albert Hall, Pontins and the Royal National Eisteddfod.

The band meets at the band room on Mondays and Fridays, and there is a Junior Section that gathers on a Thursday. The conductor is Adrian Hill B.A., L.R.A.M., who travels twice weekly from Yate, near Bristol, the bandmaster Brian Reynolds and chairman Doug Davies.

161. Markham & District Colliery Silver Prize Band, Welsh champions 1968. Back row: W. Hamer, H. Thomas, R. Jenkins, E. Harris, S. Lewis, R. Kelly. Middle row: A. Davies (sec.), J. Cornish, M. Powell, A. Coates, M. Davies, C. Powell, D.T. Price, G. Morgan, A. Lewis, W. Charles, J. Childs, D. Hamer, E. Kelly, M. Jago, R. Simmonds, B. Reynolds, D. Hendy. Front row: G. Evans, T. Pritchard, G. Price, D. Davies, P. Roberts, H. Morgan, J. Evans, R. Hamer.

162. Part of the mixed choir for a concert at the Central Methodist Church in the 1950's. The conductor is Mr. Cunningham.

163. The cast of Blackwood Little Theatre's production of The Little Foxes in 1959. Standing: Roy Fidler, Elvert Morgan, Cecil Caffull, Russell Bennett, Gwyn Beard, Henry Lewis, Clarice Lewis. Seated: Margaret Jones, Dilys Meredith, Marjorie James.

164. Celebrations in Stanley Street, Blackwood, in 1945, to mark the cessation of hostilities.

165. Celebrations at Blackwood to mark the Coronation of Queen Elizabeth II in 1953. This Cefn Road party was held in a Nissen hut on the present day site of Derwen Close.

166. Part of a jazz band parade passing along the south end of Blackwood High Street in the early 1960's.

167. A Fashion Show in the Church Hall by the staff of Jones and Richards in the early 1950's. Left to right: Val Hutchins, Dorothy Magness, Hilary Baker, Charlotte Powell, Eileen Lewis, Anne Blount, Brenda Harris, Beryl Williams, Brenda Ruck, Phyllis Filer.

168. Mrs Charlotte Powell receiving the cup from the chairman of Blackwood Welfare Institute on the occasion of winning first prize at their Drama Festival in the early 1960's. Left to right: Grove Bennett, Jerry Triplett, Giles Jones, Granville Parfitt, Charlotte Powell, Cam Bennett, Jim Davies, Ernie Jones.

169. A carnival float on Blackwood High Street c. 1950. The three Welsh ladies with their backs to the cab are left to right: Mrs Bosley, Mrs Sullivan and Mrs Dredge (Senior). Mrs Parfitt is facing the camera. The bars on the far side of the road were part of the 'bus stands before the days of the 'bus station.

170. Judges in the Blackwood Chamber of Trade Baby Competition, 1950. Left to right: Mr. L. Brown, Mrs. Jenny James, Mr. Lloyd, Mrs B. Parsons, Mr. C. Bennett.

171. Victory celebrations at Albion Terrace, Blackwood, in the summer of 1945. Mr. Gibbs sits in the centre. Behind, to the right, is 'The Hut', the home of Blackwood Dramatic Society until they purchased 'The Little Theatre'.

172. The West Mon. Omnibus Company's staff outing to Cheddar in 1930.

173. A group of Blackwood residents enjoying a day out in Porthcawl (where else!) in 1928. Behind them is their transport; a 'short lion' 'bus, which had a door at the back.

174. Argoed Carnival, c. 1966, as they progress north along the New Road.

175. Members of Blackwood Boys' Brigade First Company receiving their Queen's Badges from the Mayor of Islwyn, 1977-78. Donald Coleman (President of the Boys' Brigade for Wales), Ian Hemmings, Mark Thomas, Jeff Barrington (B.B. Welsh Secretary), Simon Morgan, Alfred Hudson (B.B. Gen. Sec. United Kingdom), The Mayor C.C. Butler, Dean Powell, John Elston, Kevin Thomas.

CHAPTER 7

People and Organisations

176. A group of young men meeting in the woods near the Jug and Bottle pit at Libanus in 1912.

177. The officers and committee members at the opening of the Markham Welfare Institute in 1926.

178. Jeanette Watson, with members of the Blackwood branch, at the Area St. John's Ambulance competitions in Cardiff, c. 1964.

179. Members of Blackwood Conservative Club outside the Masonic Hall in the early 1950's. Mr. John Lewis (with stick) is in the centre while Mr. & Mrs Cliff Slade, the steward and stewardess, are standing at the back.

180. The crew from Cefn Fforest Fire Station who won the Divisional Fire Fighting competition 1st September 1956. They are pictured in front of the County No. 10 Commer fire engine supplied by Buttons of Pengam. The tender was equipped with a 35 foot ladder, carried 400 gallons of water and was capable of pumping 400 gallons per minute when connected to a water supply. It normally carried a crew of five: a sub officer, leading fireman and three fireman. Standing left to right: R. Lurvey, I. Davies, R. Williams, H. Clovelly, D. Owen, K. Bidder, V. Reed, W. Prestidge, R. Morgan. Seated: W. Gregory, Leading fireman D. Curtis, R. Lloyd, Station Officer D. Close, Sub. Officer D. Thomas, Leading fireman K. Pritchard, D. Evans.

181. Members of a knitting group that used to knit for the forces during the war. Standing: Mrs M. Davies, Mrs S. Davies, Mrs S. Davies, Mrs O. Vaughan, Mrs Tudor Evans, Mrs C. Rees, Mrs E. Davies, Mrs E. Jones, Mrs B. Jones. Seated: Mrs R. Watkins, Miss Edmunds, Mrs E. Lewis, Mrs V. Jones.

182. Blackwood Lodge of the Loyal Order of Moose photographed in the grounds of the Woodbine Club, c. 1950. Back row: Unknown, Billy Constance, Ivor Haines, Frank Withers, Reg Davies, W. Dodd, John Lambert, Basil Lewis, A. Beard, Len Jones, Richard Davies, Cyril Morgan, Charlie Dodd. Third row: Jack Brown, Jack Maquire, Joe Walker, Harold West, Jack Griffiths, J. Lewis, A. Brown, Jack Jones, Unknown.

183. No. 1 Company Blackwood Boys' Brigade at the centenary celebrations, 4th October 1983.

Second row: Arthur Thomas, D. Lewis, B. Phillips, W. Lewis, Cyril Davies, Jack Pritchard, B. Probert, Charlie Hughes, Gron Lewis, Unknown, Bryn Wilkins, Bert Annette, Charlie Price, Reg James, Frank Jordan. Seated: Ike Hunt, P. Hill, Unknown, Hughie Hughes, Charlie Vaughan, Carter West, Tom Brown, Wil Hopkins, G. Morgan, Evan Williams, Bob Rowe, P. Lewis, Ivan Berry, L.J. Davies, Sil Evans, Unknown.

184. A Women's Institute visit to the Houses of Parliament in the 1950's.

185. The committee for Blackwood Shopping Week, c. 1950. Standing: Mr. David Prosser, Mr. Tom Lambert, Mr. Ganes, Mr. Len Brown, Mr. Ron Edwards. Mr. Lloyd (station master), Mr. C. Bennett. Seated: Unknown, Mr. Hill, Mrs Templeman, Mr. Tidal Parsons, Unknown, Mr. Les Evans, Mr. V. Croker, Mr. Jordan.

186. A gathering of Red Cross members in the 1950's.

187. Mrs D. Chaston entertaining a group of NSPCC workers in the grounds of Rock House c. 1950. Standing: Mrs Goddard, Mrs Salter, Unknown, Mrs C. Onions, Mrs F. Woodward, Dr. Woods, Mrs Eva Holsgrove, Unknown, Mrs Mal Brown, Mrs E. Edwards, Mrs G. Jones, Mrs A. Bennett, Mrs Davies, an NSPCC official, Mrs E. Jones, Mrs F.E. Williams. Seated: Mrs P. Woodward, Mrs E. Parker, an NSPCC official, Mrs D. Chaston, Clerk to the Police, Mrs J. Vranch, Mrs Chaston senior.

188. Members of the committee of Bedwellty Agricultural Society's Dog Section, in the 1950's.

CHAPTER 8

Transport, Trade and Industry

189 & 190. Tredegar Junction Station on the London and North Western Railway Line. This station was later known as the Pontllanfraith Top Station. The line ran north to Nantybwch via Tredegar.

191. Blackwood Railway Station after the platform had been extended in 1912. The white building in the centre is the Carpenter's Arms, a public house much frequented by the 'thinking men' of the town. As far back as 1806 a friendly society for women, known as the Faithful Friends, used to meet regularly here. To the right, in Station Row, is Walter's grocery shop. The Drill Hall is behind the signal box. Very little of this scene remains today.

192. Blackwood Railway Station in 1905.

193. Oakdale Colliery, Blackwood in the 1950's. This colliery was opened in 1908 by the Oakdale Navigation Company, a subsidiary of the Tredegar Iron and Coal Company. At its zenith it was producing a million tons of coal a year with manpower of 2000. When Markham Colliery was closed in 1979 its underground workings were joined to those of Oakdale. The same happened to the Celynen North Colliery, Newbridge, underground workings in 1981. In spite of massive investment unforeseen circumstances led to Oakdale Colliery being closed in 1990. This concluded coalmining in Gwent after a period in excess of 200 years.

194. The three shafts of Oakdale Colliery, c. 1914.

195. Five teenage miners at Oakdale Colliery, c. 1928. They are left to right: Ossie Prosser, Jack Morris, Tiger Thomas and in front, Jumbo Lewis and Harry Matthews. Fourteen-year-old boys started work on 'days' but when they reached their sixteenth birthday were allowed to work 'afternoons'.

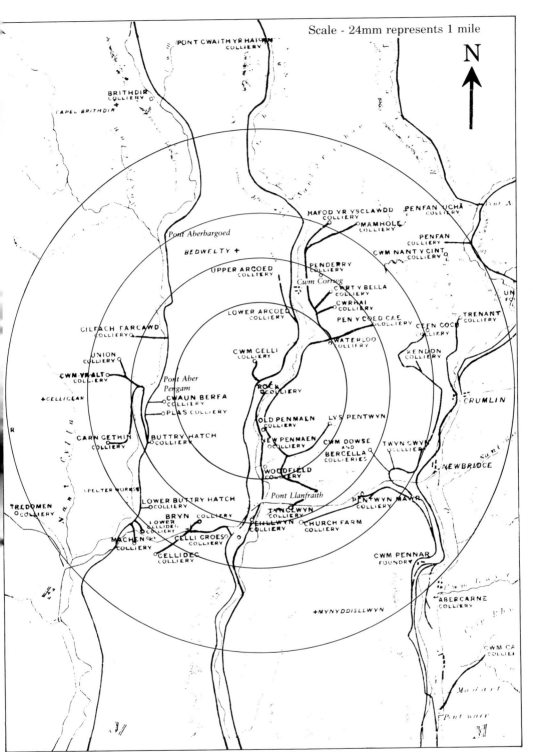

196. Part of John Prujean's Mining Map of the Ironworks and Collieries of Monmouthshire, dated 1843. It shows that at this time there were more than thirty collieries or levels within two and a half miles of the centre of Blackwood. The deep mines such as Oakdale, Wyllie and Markham were still to come.

197. Markham Colliery in 1918. This colliery, named after Arthur Markham, the company chairman, was opened by a subsidiary company of the Tredegar Iron & Coal Company, in 1912. At its height it was producing in excess of a quarter of a million tons of coal a year. It was linked to Oakdale in 1979 and closed in 1985.

198. Nine Mile Point Colliery, Cwmfelinfach (the valley with the little mill), 1950, from the south west.

199. Llanover Colliery, Argoed. This colliery, the ruins of which are still visible from the Tredegar road, together with nearby Abernant, was worked by the Bargoed Coal Company. It closed in the 1920's but was subsequently used as a pumping station for Oakdale.

200. Frank Love, mining engineer, with his pony outside Primrose Colliery at the Rock, Blackwood, in August 1937.

201. Budd's Colliery, Blackwood, in the early 1950's. Formerly known as the New Rock Colliery, this small deep mine employed about seventy men in the early 1950's and produced 15-16,000 tons of house gas, bunker and industrial coals, a year. The colliery closed on 14th June 1957. Although the Bedwellty and Mynyddislwyn Farmers' Association held shows from 1873, the first show of the Bedwellty Agricultural Society was held on this site on Thursday 18th October 1877. Adjacent fields (Pentwyn Avenue) and the Drill Hall were also used. The second show, held on the same site on 12th September 1878 was completely overshadowed by a disaster that had occurred on the previous day. An explosion at Abercarn Colliery had resulted in the death of 268 miners.

202. A renovated coal wagon of the type that would have been used in these valleys for transporting coal to the docks at Newport.

203. Tom Brown's Foundry. This general foundry was opened in c. 1913 and worked until the 1980's, soon after which Gibbon Tool Hire took over the site. The large area at the front was a quarry which the council rented to dump household refuse. When the ground was level it was covered with tarmac and used as a 'bus park by the West Mon. Bus Company.

204. Britannia Colliery, Pengam. This colliery was sunk c. 1912 and was the first colliery in the country to be operated by electricity generated on site by the Colliery Company. The village of Cefn Fforest, at first called Pengam Garden Village, was built to provide housing for the workforce at this colliery.

205. Mr. J.F. Chappell, one of the grand old businessmen of Blackwood, pictured in the early part of the century, after completing a short walk along Blackwood High Street at 90 years of age. Mr. Chappell had a grocery business (where Granada stands at present), and an adjacent sweet-shop, but owned the whole block. The sweetshop is now an estate agents. Fred Chappell was a member of the first Board of Managers, a committee formed as a consequence of the 1870 Education Act, and created when it was decided to set up the first state school in Blackwood at the Drill Hall. This school opened its doors to 73 pupils, only one of whom could multiply simple numbers, on 15th September 1873. Miss Emily Green of Bradford-on-Avon was the first mistress. She was appointed by the Board of Managers, chaired by Captain Edmund Williams of Maesrhuyddyd.

206. Tommy, pulling Smith & Sons bread cart at Cwmgelli Villas, Blackwood, in 1928. The iron rails behind the cart were used to bring coal from the Gelli Dowyllt level to the main line.

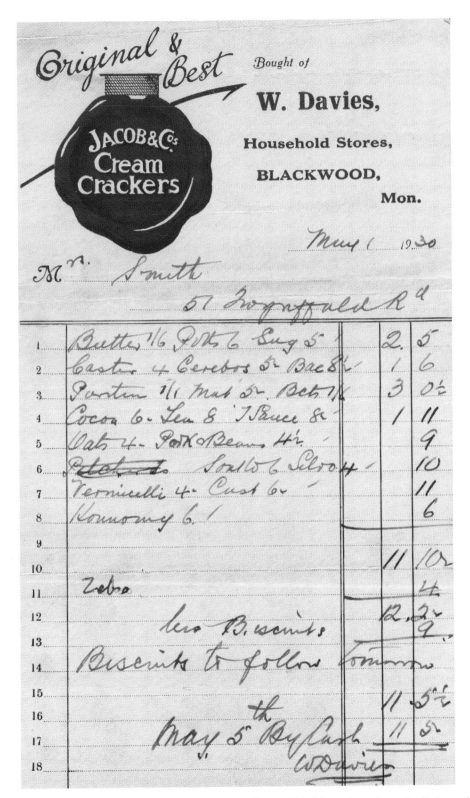

207. A typical bill for the groceries for a week in 1930. Note the prices. A 2lb bag of sugar 5d (c 2p), a box of Cerebos salt $5^{1}/_{2}$d (c 2p), $^{1}/_{2}$lb bacon $8^{1}/_{2}$d ($2^{1}/_{2}$p), a tin of cocoa 6d ($2^{1}/_{2}$p), a box of porridge oats 4d ($1^{1}/_{2}$p) etc. The price included delivery and a special errand the following day to deliver the biscuits!

208. Richard Morris' business premises on Blackwood High Street at the turn of the century. Richard Morris had arrived in Blackwood in 1836 to work for Roger Davies, his uncle. Eventually he took over the business and ran it until the turn of the century. He died in 1912 at the age of 91. He was a most go-ahead businessman and was instrumental in bringing street lighting to the village. The *Star of Gwent* on 17th January 1857 reported that Mr. Morris 'has erected a small retort and gasometer behind his place of business and manufactures gas sufficient for his own and three or four of his neighbours' use'. In 1990 Tidals Stores occupy the outfitting and drapery section; while Rowlands the newsagent is in the section marked Grocer and Provisions.

209. Jones & Richards' window, one Christmas in the 1950's. The drapery and millinery business known as Jones & Richards was created by Mr. Bill Jones and Miss Richards, both of whom had previously been employed by A.P. Hughes & Co., The Blackwood Drapers. During its many years of service to the community Jones & Richards was well known for its courteous staff, friendly atmosphere and, above all, 'Value for money'. Bill Jones had come to Blackwood from Cilycwm, a small village 4 miles north of Llandovery. Apart from his entreprenurial skills he was an active member of numerous local organisations and societies.

210. Coleman & Son, High Street, Blackwood, c. 1920. This family business, selling fruit, vegetables, fish and game, served the public as long as any other outlet on the High Street.

211. The staff at Trevor Griffiths the solicitor, c. 1920. Mr. Trevor Griffiths is in the centre wearing a trilby and Mr. Ted Williams, later to form his own practice, in a straw hat on the left. They were the leading solicitors in the town at the time, and the origin of their building is interesting. Mr. Morris (where Tidals is now) and Mr. Edmunds (who had a house on Woolworths site) were two businessmen who had little love for each other. Morris erected the building (now used by Leslie Davies, solicitors) as a store and granary to obstruct the view from Edmunds' house. For decades the building was known as 'spiteful corner'.

212. The butcher's shop of Woodward & Son on Blackwood High Street in 1922. This building was erected c. 1830 and was known as The Yew Tree Inn. For a time it was the home of Zephaniah Williams, one of the Chartist leaders. In 1854 it became a butcher's shop. Two of the windows at the back of the house were blocked up to avoid paying the window tax. There was also a stone mounting block in front for the use of the horse riding customers. Woolley's the florist and fruiterer stands on this site today.

213. The Christmas display of Woodward & Son in 1927.

214. Two pages of adverts illustrating the businesses in the town in 1919.

117

215. Alice Beatson and Julie Conti outside Conti's Cafe, c. 1928. This cafe, situated two shops north of Newbridge House at the bottom of Pentwyn Hill, Blackwood, closed in the 1950's. Mr. Conti was one of the many Italians who came to the South Wales valleys from the Italian village of Bardi. No valley town was complete without such a cafe.

216. Bryn Lewis provides general transport in the Blackwood area c. 1920.

217. The new Tredegar Cooperative Society store at Blackwood on the day it was opened in January 1963. The store is now called Belle Vue Discount.

218. Committee members and officials of the Tredegar Industrial and Provident Society on the occasion of the opening of the new Tredegar Cooperative Society store at Blackwood on 23rd January 1963. Centre front is County Councillor Lewis Lewis wearing two overcoats, illustrating how cold it was on that January day.

219. An early 1930's West Mon 'bus. Its driver, Bert Waygood and conductor, Eb Crewe are enjoying a break outside the Hanbury cinema, Bargoed before returning to Blackwood via Pengam. The West Mon Omnibus Company was formed by Act of Parliament on 28th June 1933 for the purpose of providing and running omnibuses within the areas mentioned in the act but with the prime object of serving the population in the parishes of Bedwellty and Mynyddislwyn. The board was to consist of 9 members, 6 from Bedwellty and 3 from Mynyddislwyn. The composition of the board was to change in proportion to the total rateable value of the two parishes. The company was based at Blackwood and limited to 30 'buses. It functioned until the boundary changes created the Borough of Islwyn, when it became Islwyn Transport, the 'bus company of Islwyn Borough Council.

220. The Morris van that served Smith & Sons, Bakers and Confectioners, Blackwood, c. 1930. This van, which superseded their horse and cart, had solid iron wheels and a thermometer on the bonnet that was readable from the driver's cab.